CHINA
IN OLD PHOTOGRAPHS
1860-1910

BURTON F. BEERS

CHINA
IN OLD PHOTOGRAPHS
1860-1910

CHARLES SCRIBNER'S SONS / NEW YORK

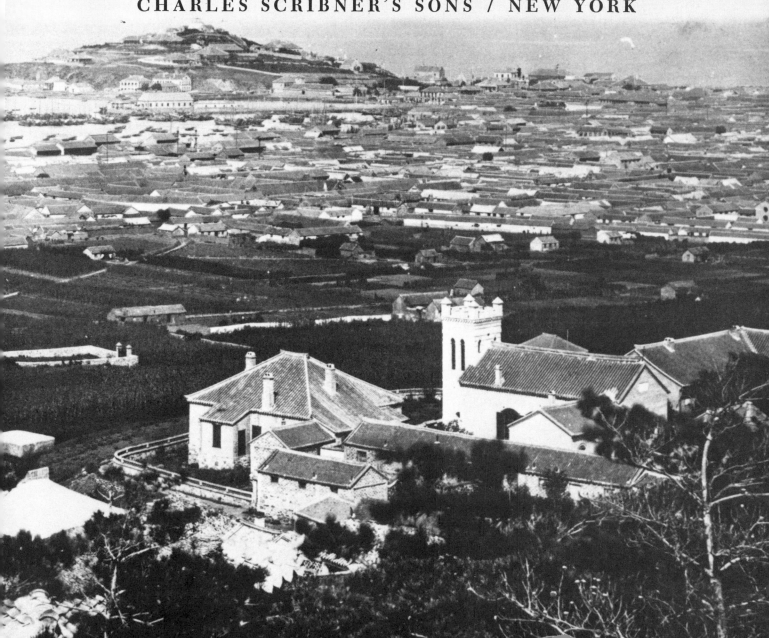

Library of Congress Cataloging in Publication Data

Beers, Burton F.
    China in old photographs, 1860-1910.

    Selected from the collection of the Museum of
the American China Trade in Milton, Mass.
    1. China—Description and travel—To 1900—
Views. 2. China—Description and travel—1901-
1948—Views. I. Museum of the American China
Trade. II. Title.
DS709.B43   951'.0022'2   78-13220
ISBN 0-684-15651-2

10-23-78

Title page. Amoy, located on the southeast coast, was one of the five ports opened to Western residence and trade after China's defeat in her first war with Great Britain, which lasted from 1839 to 1841. The excellence of the city's harbor and the volume of Chinese trade conducted there promised that Amoy would become a center for trade with the West. Christian missionaries went there (note the substantial church on the right), as did some foreign merchants. However, except for times when Amoy served as a point of departure for coolie "contract labor" (a nice name for a practice that approached slavery), the city did not attain the importance in foreign trade that had been anticipated.

FOR MY TEACHER AND COLLEAGUE,

PAUL H. CLYDE

A PIONEERING HISTORIAN WHOSE RESEARCH

MARKED A BEGINNING IN AMERICAN

STUDIES OF ASIA

CONTENTS

PREFACE

THE Museum of the American China Trade in Milton, Massachusetts, has assembled an unsurpassed collection that focuses on America's commercial and cultural relations with China from colonial times to the end of the age of sail. Located in the Captain Robert Bennet Forbes House and the Amos Holbrook House, the museum exhibits China-trade paintings, porcelains, silver, furniture, and fancy goods. Here too one finds a large and growing collection of books, manuscripts, and documents that are an indispensable resource for historical research on the tea, silk, opium trades, and the China trade in general.

The photographs in this volume were selected from more than two thousand in the museum's files, and more than two-thirds of them were taken by anonymous photographers. Most of the museum's picture collection dates from the beginnings of photography in China during the 1850s to the collapse of China's last dynasty in 1911. In general, the photographs reflect the interests and tastes of the Americans who brought them home along with other treasures of their stay in China. What one finds are superb pictures of old China itself and of an expanding Western presence on the China coast.

Since early pictures of China are rare, and those that have survived were closeted in private collections, only a few privileged people have ever seen such photographs. They are made available here because the museum is deeply committed to expanding the use of its resources to improve understanding of the China trade legacy.

Indeed, the idea of publishing this book originated with the museum's talented and scholarly staff. It was M. Greer Hardwicke who first organized the pictures and catalogued them, thereby giving us access to the collection. The museum's Associate Director, Francis R. Carpenter, has worked closely with me all along the way. His support of my efforts has been so generous and his advice so helpful that it is no exaggeration to say that he deserves much of the credit for the book. Nor would this volume have been possible without the unflagging support of the museum's director, Paul E. Molitor, Jr., and its founder-curator, H. A. Crosby Forbes.

My ultimate debt, of course, is to those American families who preserved these invaluable photographs and deposited them at the Museum of the American China Trade.

Finally, to Norman Kotker and Wendy Afton Rieder of Charles Scribner's Sons I extend thanks for their patience and expert guidance. They are model editors.

BURTON F. BEERS

PERSPECTIVES:
Looking at Old Photographs

Windows on Our Minds

AMERICANS have never been quite sure what to believe about China. Our opinions have shifted about and have run to extremes. Within recent memory, during the years from World War II to Richard Nixon's much publicized presidential trip to Peking in 1972, the nation's China policy encouraged the public to view the Chinese successively as loyal allies fighting at our side in democracy's cause, as mindless "blue ants" that had fallen for totalitarian rule, and as patriotic revolutionaries with whom, however much we might differ on ideology, accommodation was possible. In effect, Americans were supplied with a new image of China every decade or so.

The pace was truly dizzying, but the ambiguities in American opinion were not new. Earlier generations seem to have alternated between lauding the Chinese and laying them low. Thomas Jefferson, for example, gleaned from his reading that China was to be admired as the seat of a model agrarian society. On the other hand, S. Wells Williams, an able missionary who only a few years after Jefferson's time was to experience the frustrations of evangelizing an unreceptive people, complained that

> it is much easier loving the heathen in the abstract than in the concrete encompassed as they are in such dirty bodies, speaking forth their foul language and vile natures exhibiting every evidence of depravity.[1]

The American tendency to be of several minds about China is reflected in the pictures printed in this book. These photographs once were a portion of the memorabilia brought back to the United States by those who had traveled or lived in China. Some photographs are more than 120 years old, dating nearly to the time of China's first defeat by British forces, in 1841. All the rest were made before the collapse of China's ruling Ch'ing Dynasty in 1911. To Americans intrepid enough to have made the trip, the China of these years presented richly varied experiences that invited judgments comparing Confucian and Western civilizations on all manner of things—life-styles, religions, culinary tastes, architectural designs, or technologies. We have here a photographic record that not only reveals how old China looked but also suggests the disparate ways Americans reacted to it.

Anyone looking through files of these old photographs can recapture at least some of China's enormous appeal to outsiders. For one thing, it was a land of unsurpassed natural beauty, and Western photographers, like countless generations of native landscape painters, never tired of picturing rugged mountains, great river gorges, or a peasantry living close to the forces of nature. An appreciation, too, for the accomplishments of a seemingly timeless civilization is evident in the many pictures (both with and without foreign tourists) of monuments from much earlier times: the Great Wall, Peking's Imperial City, or the giant statues lining the paths to the Ming tombs. Moreover, the pictures of everyday life— Chinese tending their shops, working their fields, or looking after their children—suggest an appreciation for China that transcended the "quaintness" of her ways. The Chinese might be different, but they did embrace values to which Americans could warm.

Nor should we miss in these photographs evidence of another idea that Americans were fond of articulating: China was a very special place because she offered so many opportunities that could be of reciprocal advantage. The American business community, for example, liked to think of the mutual benefits that would flow from penetration of the China market. China was said to be in dire need of a modern commercial and industrial system that would overcome her poverty, and Americans assumed that, as citizens of the most dynamic Western nation, they were superbly equipped to teach the Chinese how to build it. Thus the lure of prospective profits was reinforced by the idea that business would contribute to permanent improvements in Chinese life. In like manner, Christian missions were thought to offer American churches dual opportunities, leading the Chinese to salvation while offering them ideas that would transform their secular world. Although Americans of the 1970s may think it incredible that an earlier generation could have been so confident of their nation's capacity to determine the destiny of others, we should not doubt the power of these ideas to color what Americans saw in China. Scenes depicting a Western presence—even those of a Western officer standing guard over Chinese prisoners in Shanghai, a Christian church in an old Chinese burial ground, or Western troops parading on Chinese soil —were not recorded as evidence of unwarranted foreign intervention. Rather, they were viewed at the time as images of friendship, service, and sacrifice.

Once Americans were actually inside China, however, they not infrequently discovered that their leadership was rejected. Chinese were wedded to their own ways and were unwilling to admit that outsiders might have better ones. In these circumstances, it was easy to lose sight of China's charm and to interpret as sheer perversity what some had thought was quaint. Thus, mixed with photographs that make old China glow are those of assorted brutalities: maltreatment of even petty criminals, coolies breaking their bodies with inhuman tasks, and deformities caused by binding women's feet. Indeed, when outsiders were disposed to be critical, even small matters could feed their indignation. An American who had dismally failed in efforts to persuade some Chinese of the value of a power saw noted on his snapshot of two coolies cutting a board from a huge log by hand that the sawdust did not even come out of the "right" side of the log. Close encounters across cultural frontiers, it seems, did not always improve international understanding.

Photography Comes to China

IT will not do, however, to stress too much the impact of American attitudes on the kinds of photographs that were collected and preserved. The nature of the pictures we have inherited was probably influenced even more by photography's slow start in China. By the 1850s, armchair travelers in Europe and America were enjoying views of Niagara Falls, the Alps, Rome, and the pyramids through the magic of stereopticon slides. Even India could be visited vicariously as British colonials turned to photography as a hobby. Yet photographs of China were seen by only a privileged few. Two daguerreotypists attached to Commodore Matthew C. Perry's naval expedition (1852–54) made pictures in the vicinity of Hong Kong and Canton when the American fleet was in Chinese waters on its way to Japan. Since daguerreotypes could not be duplicated as photographic prints, these pictures—the first known to have been made in China—were turned into steel-engraved reproductions and circulated as illustrations of the official account of the Perry expedition.[2]

Some ten years later John Thomson, a Scotsman who was to become one of the most famous early photographers, journeyed more than four thousand miles along China's coast and into the interior taking hundreds of pictures. A portion of these were duplicated on photographic paper and pasted into an expensive four-volume book that described Thomson's travels.[3] A still smaller number were copied by the steel-engraving process and printed in a more popular book that covered all of Thomson's ten-year stay in Southeast Asia and China.[4]

Meanwhile another European, Felice Beato, marched with British and French forces from the China coast to Peking during the last campaign of the Arrow War (1858–60). He photographed the destruction of China's Taku forts and the imperial government's summer palace. Some copies of Beato's work may have been sold in cities frequented by Westerners along the China coast, but they do not appear to have been circulated much in Europe or America. Finally, by the late 1850s shops in the coastal cities were selling some *cartes de visite* (precursors of postcards), which illustrated native types or showed Chinese at work. These were generally made by photographers of so little note that their names have been lost.

In its beginnings, photography was an exclusively Western art, which explains the rarity of old photographs from China. During photography's very earliest years—before 1860—Westerners quite literally had only toeholds on China's coast. Until 1842 virtually all intercourse between China and the West was funneled through an area no larger than fifteen acres, on the waterfront of Canton in southeastern China. Five coastal cities, including Canton, were opened to foreign residence and trade in 1842, as a concession to the force of British arms, but the rest of the country remained off-limits until a second Chinese defeat in the Arrow War. Even with these legal dispensations, Westerners ordinarily did not venture far into China unless they were businessmen or missionaries. China lacked the kind of transportation system and tourist facilities common in Western Europe and the United States. Moreover, the foreign traveler could not be certain of a welcome wherever he went.

All these limitations were compounded for the early photographer by the technology of his profession. Until about 1880, when modern film was introduced and cameras were revolutionized, cameras were invariably bulky and required an amazing array of auxiliary equipment. Except when daguerreotypes were used, exposures were made on heavy glass plates, which were themselves no small items to carry about. At first these plates were coated just before exposure with an emulsion made with fresh egg whites. The subsequent substitution of a collodion-on-glass process, which eliminated the need for carrying along cases of heavily packed eggs, made the camera a bit more portable and provided an additional advantage in faster exposure. Even so, the photographer on the move still carried boxes of plates, a portable darkroom, bottles of chemicals, and, not infrequently, his own water supply. In another part of the world, Roger Fenton, the photographer who taught Felice Beato his trade, solved the logistical problems of following the troops in the Crimean War by fitting out a darkroom and luggage carrier on a sizable horse-drawn wagon. Photographers in China made short trips from their studios, using sedan chairs, wheelbarrows, or springless wagons. On longer journeys, boats were usually the only practical vehicles. Faced with these circumstances, few photographers traveled as much as Beato or Thomson.

The hazards, great and small, that Thomson encountered

along the way became, in the telling, part of the romance of his travels. Two small boats, which on their upstream course were sailed, poled, or hauled against the current, transported Thomson, his companion, and their gear some twelve hundred miles up the Yangtze River. Some days were enlivened by meetings with Chinese, or boating mishaps. Others were just tedious. Thomson's quarters on the little boat were cramped, and his crew was best appreciated from a distance. Thomson recalled that "the skipper and his spouse smoked stale tobacco half through the night, and the fumes came through the bulkhead and filled my sleeping bunk. . . . The boatmen were a miserable lot. They neither changed their clothes nor washed their bodies during the entire trip. . . . Their clothes were padded with cotton, and formed their habiliments by day and their bedding by night. Poor souls, how they crept together, and huddled into the hold; and what an odor arose from their retreat in the morning, for they had smoked themselves to sleep with tobacco, or those of them who could afford it, with opium. It was always a difficult matter to get them up and out on deck to face the cold. . . . But the voice [of the boatman's wife] is equal to the occasion. She shakes those sluggards from their rest with her strident cries; she stamps her cabin, and 'slings slang' at them like the foulest missiles."[5] It is not surprising that the first pictures from China were made mostly in the coastal cities or along the more accessible rivers and canals.

The impact of technological innovation is evident in these pictures. Not only are there more photographs from the years after simpler cameras were introduced in the 1880s, but modern films made snapshots a reality. Whereas the earliest pictures from China ran heavily to landscapes and stilted poses, those of the late nineteenth century often achieved the spontaneity of a candid shot. Yet an improved technology or even legal access to the hinterland did not solve problems arising from Chinese suspicions of outsiders with cameras. Thomson was unusually successful in persuading some Chinese to pose by paying them small sums. Even then he often felt threatened, as he wrote: "Carrying out my task involved both difficulty and danger. In many places there were those who had never set eyes on a pale-faced stranger; and the literati, or educated classes, had fostered a notion amongst such as these, that, while evil spirits of every kind were carefully to be shunned, none ought to be so strictly avoided as the 'Fan Qui' or 'Foreign Devil,' who assumed human shape. . . . I therefore frequently enjoyed the reputation of being a dangerous geomancer, and my camera was held to be a dark mysterious instrument."[6]

Like other photographers, Thomson discovered that Chinese suspicions were most intense in the regions where the native population and foreigners were in closest contact. By the 1890s, as the Western presence became quite obtrusive, antiforeign riots were common. In these circumstances, photographers, particularly the amateurs who were increasingly important as a source of pictures, often had difficulty getting close enough to Chinese to portray the more intimate aspects of their lives.

Photography as a Historical Record

WE should approach these photographs with the understanding that they catch old China in decline. Part of China's troubles came from an increasingly incompetent government. The Manchus, who were to rule as the Ch'ing Dynasty, had invaded China from a northeastern borderland, defeated the native Chinese Mings, and established their own government in 1644. They governed ably at first, winning support from China's populace. But, as had all previous dynasties, the Ch'ing government in time sagged under its own weight and fatigue. The first popular uprisings were scattered and vulnerable to the government's counterattack. In the 1850s, however, a group known as the T'ai-p'ings started an uprising that spread over much of central China. Soon there were formidable upheavals in other regions. After fourteen years and the death of millions of Chinese, the rebellions were snuffed out, but the Ch'ing Dynasty had been grievously hurt.

An honored Chinese theory held that when a dynasty fell, another would eventually take its place and life would go on much as before. China in rebellion, however, was suffering from fundamental economic and social troubles that promised to force unprecedented change. Population growth, for example, was threatening to outrun production of the essentials of life. It was no longer possible to accommodate the increasing numbers of people by opening additional land. Without new technology, expanded production was not possible. In consequence, tradition came under fire. Sometimes the call for better ways came from the Chinese literati, whose positions of leadership, ironically, were built on their identification with Confucian learning. Sometimes it came from rebels, such as those among the T'ai-p'ings who called for a basic reordering of social and economic institutions. Even the imperial government, which was casting about for ways to save itself, endorsed reform in the 1860s and again in the first decade of the twentieth century. Little was accomplished in the era covered by these pictures. Nevertheless, the early revolutionary stirrings are worth noting here because they are indicative of how serious old China's problems were.

Worse still, these domestic problems affected the Chinese at the very time that their international fortunes were changing. From its inception, Chinese civilization had dominated East Asia. Moreover, except for the successful invasions of the Mongols and Manchus, China had held the upper hand in dealings with its neighbors. China's defeat in its first war with Great Britain and its concessions to the British (and subsequently to other powers) in the treaty signed in 1842 marked the beginnings of a shift in the balance of power. For the next century, China was thrown onto the defensive against foreign powers.

China's foreign problems were by no means entirely the product of its own declining fortunes. China was confronted by a Western world whose reach was extending over the entire globe and later by an increasingly strong Japan. For many years China had experienced no great difficulties in managing visitors from the West. Catholic missionaries had been allowed to work among Chinese in the sixteenth and seventeenth centuries, only to be banished from the empire when they challenged Peking's authority; Russians approaching along Asia's inner frontiers were controlled by treaties setting terms on which they might trade with Chinese; and Western Europeans and Americans were permitted to land only at Macao and Canton and to deal with Chinese as Peking prescribed. This Chinese superiority reflected the realities of power. Nearly a century before the Spanish monarchy financed Columbus's voyages, the Ming court sent a fleet of sixty-two seagoing junks with twenty-eight thousand men to the mouth of the Persian Gulf. During the next two or three centuries, however, the nations of the West amassed power while China remained relatively static. As a result, the British, who had earlier tamely acceded to the requirement that they trade solely at Canton, were able to put ten thousand men with modern arms on the China coast in the 1840s. The Chinese could not stop the British then, and they were helpless when British and French forces marched into Peking in 1860, laying waste to buildings that symbolized the might of the Celestial Empire.

As a fledgling power, the United States could do little either to encourage the established powers or to restrain them as China was reduced to a semicolonial status, but American citizens figured importantly in the growing foreign presence in China. The graceful clipper ships, whose speed made them the flagships of the tea and opium trade during the first half of the nineteenth century, symbolized the American stake in China. Between 1870 and 1900 the number of American firms doing business in China rose from 50 to 81, a growth that would continue until there were 556 firms in 1930. The expansion of American missionary activities was even more dramatic: in 1870 some 200 missionaries were supported by 12 American missionary societies; in 1900 about 1,000 missionaries were backed by 28 societies; and in 1930 about 3,000 missionaries represented 60 societies. Americans took the lead in introducing China to Western-style medicine and education. By 1930, 14 colleges, 180 lower schools, and 150 hospitals in China received American support. It is from the Americans serving with these expanding enterprises that we have received most of this collection of old photographs.

Given the difficulties of making pictures with early cameras, it is not surprising that the oldest photographs in these personal collections were mostly the work of professionals. Americans, like other foreigners in China, purchased pictures along with other mementos of their stays. Not until the simple camera became popular after 1880 did photograph albums begin to assume the more intimate touch of the amateur. Yet, whatever their source, these old photographs are a superb record of the China that Americans saw. This is not to say, of course, that the view of China is comprehensive or is one that Chinese might like to have presented of their country. Enough has been said about American perceptions of China and the limits imposed on early photographers to indicate that old photographs have their biases. Even so, the camera has provided us with remarkable views of the last days of China's great empire.

NOTES

1. *Missionary Herald* (Boston), XXXVIII (August 1842), p. 336.

2. Francis L. Hawks, ed., *Narrative of the Expedition of an American Squadron to the China Seas and Japan Performed in the Years 1852, 1853, and 1854, under the Command of Commodore M. C. Perry, United States Navy* . . . (New York: D. Appleton & Co., 1856), pp. 149–73. The daguerreotypes themselves have been lost.

3. J. Thomson, *Illustrations of China and Its People: A Series of Two Hundred Photographs with Letterpress Description of the Places and People Represented*, 4 vols. (London: Sampson Low, Marston, Low, and Searle, 1873).

4. J. Thomson, *The Straits of Malacca, Indo-China, and China; or Ten Years' Travels, Adventures, and Residence Abroad* (New York: Harper & Brothers, 1875). With the development of the halftone printing process toward the end of the nineteenth century, Thomson was able to print a hundred of his China pictures in a relatively inexpensive book that described again his travels in China. See Thomson, *Through China with a Camera* (Westminster: A. Constable & Co., 1898).

5. Thomson, *Straits of Malacca*, pp. 431–32.

6. Thomson, *Illustrations of China and Its People*, Introduction.

CHINA
IN OLD PHOTOGRAPHS
1860-1910

1. *Fei-lai ssu*, a Buddhist monastery on the Pearl River west of
Canton, was reputed to be the most scenic resting place in south
China. The monasteries of China, like those of Europe, frequently
offered hospitality to travelers. At *Fei-lai ssu* one could secure
lodgings, food, religious souvenirs carved from the wood of sacred
groves, and pipes of opium.

LANDSCAPES

WESTERN photographers, like generations of native landscape artists, were entranced by the rich variety of China's natural beauty. Within a vast empire, cameras might be focused on all manner of poetically composed scenes—temples nesting against rugged hills, fishermen working with their nets in picturesque waters, arched bridges crossing rural streams, or even the Great Wall winding majestically over barren wastelands. Such pictures seemed to echo a theme that ran through so many of the painted landscapes: in China, they suggested, man had mastered the supremely important art of living harmoniously with nature.

Yet the China portrayed in these photographs was a nation in trouble. Even as the camera recorded that venerable civilization's virtues, it revealed some of the sources of China's difficulties. The critical eye can see, for example, rugged hillsides that not only are scenic but also are stripped of vegetation and badly eroded. Indeed, the demand for wood was so great that a really large tree is seldom seen in these pictures. Equally great demands were imposed on cropland. Where the soil was rich and the climate favorable, fields were densely clustered, separated only by narrow footpaths. In less promising areas, terraced plots had been laboriously carved into hillsides so that no arable soil remained untilled. Reality was out of tune with the ideal. China's population had become so large that men were pressing too hard on nature's bounty.

2. John Thomson, the most talented of the Western photographers in China during the 1860s, was extraordinarily successful in capturing the distinctive qualities of Chinese landscapes.

This view of temples, paddy fields, and limestone hills arising abruptly out of the plains of southeastern China recalls the best work of native painters.

3. China's arched bridges proved endlessly fascinating to foreign visitors, who admired both their engineering and their aesthetic qualities. In setting up his camera to photograph this one, Thomson had badly frightened three old women who had been drawing water and gossiping at the edge of the river. Later the headman of the village, the edge of which can be glimpsed through the bamboo, told him that the women thought the camera was a diabolical instrument for the destruction of their homes.

4. The Yangtze River offered more than a peaceful spot to fish. As a navigable waterway stretching from China's eastern coast some thousand miles into the western interior, the river was a major commercial highway. Paths cut into the rock cliffs on either side of the river enabled teams of human "trackers" to haul heavily loaded craft upstream against surging currents.

5. With a heavy load balanced at either end of a carrying pole, a porter trudges along a north China road. The Westerner and burro on the right are part of the photographer's party.

6. Another of Thomson's pictures used the branches of an unusually large tree and small groves of bamboo to frame the view of a south China farm. Thomson's camera was not fast enough to catch the inhabitants, all of whom, except for a small child, had moved to a safe distance. The earthenware jars in the foreground were common utility vessels, probably used here to carry water from the pond.

7. *Opposite*. Pedestrian bridges, which carried no heavy traffic, could be built with curving arches that almost disappeared at the top into the walkways. The covering on this bridge was of a style said to be peculiar to Szechwan Province in western China.

8. *Below*. This temple dedicated to the Queen of Heaven, a deity worshiped by the local boating population, was located in the Min River in eastern Fukien Province. The banyan tree at right was popularly believed to be nourished by the goddess herself because the roots seemed to cling to nothing but solid stone.

9. *Overleaf*. The uniformity of China's cityscapes was in marked contrast to the variety of her landscapes. Buildings that had little space between them and were constructed of the same red brick to a uniform height of two or three stories produced relatively even skylines, broken only by an occasional temple or pagoda. This is a view of Foochow in 1870. The pagoda in the right background is presumed to be one thousand years old.

10. The Great Wall had been built in the third century B.C. as a permanent barrier protecting the agrarian Chinese from marauding, nomadic neighbors to the north. Constructed with forced labor, the wall linked a number of previously existing shorter structures and, when completed, extended some thirteen hundred miles inland from the eastern coast. Later rulers built less imposing walls to the south or north as circumstances required. The Great Wall was kept repaired until the sixteenth century. Although the wall did not stop either the Mongols or the Manchus from invading and conquering China, it enabled relatively small Chinese forces to hold off raiding parties until reinforcements arrived.

INHERITANCES

CONFUCIAN China's waning vitality was nowhere more evident than in the decay of the monuments bequeathed by one of the world's great civilizations. In Peking an embattled dynasty seemed incapable of maintaining even the symbols of its once awesome power. Visitors noted that moats surrounding city walls had been allowed to become shallow lagoons through which camel caravans waded easily. The walls themselves were defended with replicas of cannons that could not fire a shot. Outside the city the Great Wall was falling down, and the trees that had enhanced the approach to the tombs of the Ming emperors had long ago been destroyed by a populace that needed wood.

These were sorry sights, but if one may judge interest by the number of photographs of pagodas, temples, city gates, and the like that were brought home by foreign visitors, these relics had lost none of their charm. Even as old China was dying, she retained an enormous capacity to fascinate outsiders.

Pagoda at Canton 2500 Years old

11. Pagodas were photographed more frequently than any other of China's unique structures, perhaps because there were so many of them and because most were said to be very old. This one in Canton, known as the Flowery Pagoda, was said to have been built over two thousand years ago. Visitors also were drawn to pagodas, it seemed, because it was possible to climb the interior stairs of those in good repair to view the surrounding countryside.

12. *Opposite.* Pagodas might be built of brick, stone, or wood, and they varied considerably in architectural detail. Their form derived from the stupas built by India's Buddhists, but in Chinese hands it quickly lost any resemblance to the Indian originals. Eventually, much of the association between pagodas and Buddhism was lost.

13. *Below.* P'u-t'o, or Priests' Island, a Buddhist temple complex dedicated to Kuan-yin, the goddess of mercy, covered a small island near Ningpo. Since it was easy to reach from some of the principal foreign settlements, it became one of the standard stops on the visitor's itinerary.

14. *Opposite.* Buddhism became a major force in Chinese life not only as a popular religion but also as an influence on art, architecture, and even diet. Although it suffered a decline after its heyday in the T'ang Dynasty (seventh to ninth centuries A.D.), Buddhism enjoyed a new popularity in the latter years of the nineteenth century. The monks here are seen reciting prayers.

15. Foreigners might be drawn to Buddhist temples, but they seldom had kind words to say about the Buddhist faith. In most cases, the criticism reflected the visitors' own religious biases. It also is evident that visitors often did not see Buddhism at its best. The monks at P'u-t'o Monastery, for example, appear to have devoted considerable time to posing for pictures and otherwise catering to tourists. The characters engraved on the rocks are Chinese for *namah amitabha*, meaning to call the Buddha's name. Repeating the Buddha's name endlessly was held to be one way to salvation.

16. Temples were frequently carved into the sides of cliffs or fitted into caves. Buddhism produced a large number of cave temples in the north when the faith entered China, but in most of the country it was often difficult to identify a temple with a particular faith. Indeed, many villages boasted only a single temple dedicated to the *San Chiao* ("Three Religions"): Confucianism, Buddhism, and Taoism.

17. Lama Buddhism, a sect that dominated the religious life of Tibet, claimed a substantial following in north China. This monastery outside Peking, which can also be seen in picture 19, was known both as a center of the faith and as a place of unusual beauty.

18, 19. Much of Chinese sculpture is identified with religions, particularly Buddhism. Temple entrances were commonly flanked by guardian figures (*below*). Inside, animal and human figures dramatized the lessons (*opposite*). The carvings were seldom naturalistic. Yet they were persuasive representations of living things, imbued with fierceness, watchfulness, strength, agility, or whatever quality might be required.

20. *Opposite*. Memorials to holders of the title *hanlin*—the highest distinction of the Confucian scholar—stand outside a temple dedicated to Confucius. The path to this achievement began in the examination cells and ended in a test held in the presence of the emperor. Along the way these distinguished few had outdistanced hundreds of thousands of other candidates. Their reward was appointment to the highest civil posts.

21. The government erected Confucian temples throughout the empire. The greatest of these was in Peking, where the emperor led the ceremonial rites. Lesser structures like this one were found in every county. Here the local gentleman scholars held ceremonials that simultaneously honored the sage and reinforced their own claims to leadership.

22. Other impressive reminders of China's heritage were the Ming tombs near the first Ming capital at Nanking. The great gate to the tombs had five enormous portals.

23. This memorial arch was another part of the Ming tombs at Nanking.

24. Along the road to the mausoleum (in the distance) stood colossal stone figures. A later emperor named Yung-lo reproduced similar figures on an even larger scale at the base of some hills north of Peking.

25. *Left.* This composite picture made up of two photographs portrays the scale of the capital. The walls of the Imperial City can be seen running across the middle of the picture. To the left is Prospect Hill. Extending south from it, all the way to the right of the picture, is an imposing line of great throne halls with golden-tiled roofs, each one rising from a terrace of white marble.

26. *Opposite.* Peking, the seat of the ruling Ch'ing Dynasty, was laid out on a grander scale than other cities. Here shops and houses stretch out along an imperial highway leading away from the capital. Dirt was dug from the pits at the side of the road to fill potholes.

27. *Right.* Peking was a city of walls within walls. Yung-lo ordered the city to be surrounded by a wall that was forty feet high and fourteen miles around; it was entered through nine fortified gates. In the center of the city were walls, now gone, surrounding the capitol grounds, the Imperial City. Within these were the high red walls that encircled the palaces, the Forbidden City. Later another wall, a gateway of which is shown here, was built around an outer city that grew up south of the main city walls.

28. *Overleaf.* Peking's design differed markedly from that of other cities. Its main streets were wide and laid out in a grid around the imperial buildings. This was the work of the Ming emperor Yung-lo, who ordered that the capital be moved northward from Nanking in 1421. The central portion of the bridge on this Peking street was reserved for imperial traffic.

29. *Opposite.* To anyone who knew them well, Chinese cities did not all look alike. Compare, for example, the roof lines of this building in the north with the lines of the rooftops of Foochow shown in picture 9. The design of the Foochow roofs was characteristic of south China. Two-wheeled carts, such as the one seen parked here, were common to the region around Peking. The turbaned gentleman in front of the building is an Indian, probably one of the many brought by the British to serve in China as soldiers or police guarding British lives and property.

30. It was the human traffic, not the buildings, that made China's cities fascinating. When weather permitted, people swarmed into narrow streets to cook, gossip, or play. Petty merchants and food vendors hawked their wares. Sometimes street life became so heavy that pedestrian or vehicular traffic was virtually stopped. The structure seen here over the street is a memorial erected to commemorate a distinguished or particularly virtuous life.

31. Shop fronts were thrown open in the day and closed at night by means of shutters that slid along grooves. Usually, not much effort was made to display goods. Shops were given fanciful names, which were proudly inscribed on the signs outside. One simply had to remember that a place called Celestial Advantage sold table covers, chair cushions, and divans. Rooms behind the shop and overhead served as living quarters for the shopkeeper's family and his workmen.

32. *Opposite*. Except in Peking, city streets were narrow. Few were more than ten or twelve feet wide. In Canton most streets, such as the one pictured here, scarcely exceeded eight feet. Fire was a constant danger where buildings were so closely packed. Moreover, because of the absence of modern sanitary practices and adequate ventilation, the odors were overpowering to the uninitiated. Yet this density suited the Chinese, who had to move about on foot.

33. For nineteenth-century Americans, whose own country was still sparsely populated, the ever-present crowds in China were unforgettable. The laughter of the men in this picture was apparently evoked by the antics of foreigners riding a train that had stopped in a north China village.

PEOPLE

OLD China's social order scarcely resembled the ever-changing, classless, and egalitarian society to be found on the Chinese mainland today. Confucius's ideals, in contrast with Mao's, honored stability, not revolution. The ideal world, it was said, was arranged to accommodate the fundamental inequality of people. Therefore, a class system that clearly identified the gentleman scholar, the peasant farmer, the merchant, and so on was a contribution to the ordering of human affairs. Similarly helpful was recognition of distinctions that assigned places to individuals within families: age, not youth, was to be honored, and males were held to be superior to females. Society, in effect, was pictured as a gigantic jigsaw puzzle. Everyone had his own niche in the larger design, and it was imperative that each find his place and hold to it. If such ideals have little appeal now, it must be remembered that they served the Chinese for a remarkably long time. They were ideals that seemed relevant in a society that changed little from one generation to the next. Moreover, as applied in Chinese life, Confucianism theory encouraged a humane rather than an oppressive society.

The photographs made in the last half of the nineteenth century depict the old social order still in place. The visible signs of this enduring social tradition encouraged the notion that China was unchanging and unchangeable. At the turn of the century, however, these convictions had been replaced by predictions that China was entering an age of revolution. The reality, of course, was that the storm had not burst quite so suddenly. Voices claiming that the old order had outlived its usefulness and demanding fundamental social reform had been raised throughout the preceding century, but they had not been heard or had been given little weight.

34. Her distinctive hairstyle and fingernail guards mark this lady as a member of the ruling Manchus and a person of leisure. Note that Manchu women did not bind their feet as Chinese women did.

35. Bound feet were thought to enhance a woman's beauty. As the youth of these silk-garbed ladies from Amoy might suggest, the binding of feet started early in life. It was particularly common among the wealthy. Tiny feet would improve even a poor girl's chances of a good marriage, but many families could ill afford to have potentially valuable laborers crippled for life.

36. The foot on the right shows how the tight bindings over the years forced the bones down and back under the arch. To achieve these results, women endured pain and were obliged to walk with a stiff-legged gait; it was as if they were walking on their heels throughout life.

37. Gentleman scholars, such as these seated in an ornate garden, were the cream of society. This tiny elite monopolized the civil bureaucracy, claimed the highest social standing, and enjoyed the blessings of wealth. Since it was education that was presumed to make the gentleman, the offspring of the humblest peasant might theoretically move upward by mastering the Confucian classics. The reality was that the established elite tended to perpetuate itself.

38, 39. *Opposite*. These two elaborately furnished rooms illustrate what money could buy in old China. The heavy (and terribly uncomfortable) furniture, scroll paintings, and carved woodwork reflect traditional taste in interior design. Only the oil lamps are a new touch.

40. Elaborate homes were concealed behind unadorned walls. Behind this wall were probably a house and garden whose beauty provided a startling contrast with the drab street scene. Rickshas and pullers were available for hire on the streets. If a family had one of its own, most likely they would have kept it inside, not parked outside on the street like an American automobile.

41. *Below.* Even in decay, this once great country home expresses Chinese ideas of elegance and comfort. Enclosed in these buildings probably were a hall for the ancestral tablets, a schoolroom, various sitting rooms, and quarters for family, concubines, and servants. Many of the detached buildings were connected with delicately decorated covered walkways. In better times the rice paddy would have been one of several gardens.

42. *Above*. Wealth could be acquired in various ways. These rows of examination cells, however, were the only way to the most esteemed place in society. In countless tiny cubicles all over the empire, candidates steeped in the Confucian classics took examinations offered periodically by the government. Only a small number passed even the lowest level of these exams and thereby gained eligibility for appointment to a civil-service post. This fact failed to discourage the thousands who appeared whenever the examinations were held.

43. A local temple was a place for gossip as well as worship. The fortune teller seated at the table is the only person associated with temple business. The others are idlers passing the time and, perhaps, hoping for a handout. The inscriptions on the signs admonish the townspeople to behave virtuously.

44, 45. In lighter moments urban Chinese might resort to amusement parks. A tea house (*above*) offered refreshment to those who traversed the many-angled bridge. Elsewhere, men gathered about the tents of performers (*below*) to watch puppets, a magic show, or some other offering from a rich theatrical repertoire.

46. The customs-tax collector standing in the doorway had smiles for the camera, but his station was equipped with a stern warning for miscreants. Note the wooden frame propped against the wall on the collector's right. This device—known as a *cangue*—weighed twenty or thirty pounds and was fitted about the neck of those convicted of lesser crimes. Serious offenders were flogged, banished, or executed. Jails were used to hold prisoners awaiting trial, but not for punishment.

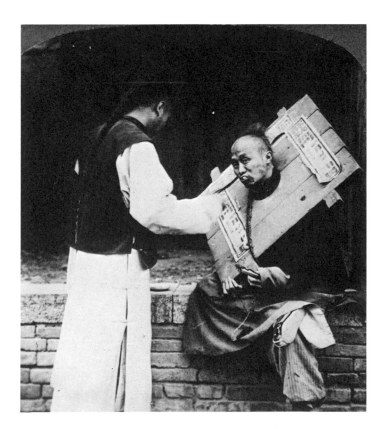

47. Once the *cangue* was in place, the wearer could not lie down or feed himself. The tags pasted on the frame give the offender's name and the reason for his humiliation.

48. Families crowding the paths along a canal appear to be celebrating a holiday.

49. *Overleaf.* Even when there wasn't reason for celebration, groups of people were usually visible everywhere engaged in some form of work.

50. Sons were more desired than daughters because they sustained the family and did not require wedding expenses. But these considerations, as this photograph of a father and daughter testify, did not prevent Chinese from loving their female offspring.

51. Children always seemed to have someone to bounce them or carry them about. This youngster, dressed in the heavy padded clothing worn during the winter months in north China, is out with an older brother.

52. The gentleman in the center wears the wispy moustache that identifies him as a person of age, one to be respected. This does not mean that he was old by our standards. In a society that was virtually devoid of modern medicine, life expectancy was somewhere around thirty years. To be sixty was to be old.

53, 54. *Left and opposite.*
Two pictures made by a commercial photographer (the man in picture 53 also appears in the background of picture 54) offer a fine opportunity to study faces, although the poses themselves are stilted. It was not unusual to see men sitting down for a smoke. Tobacco was used in China by the early sixteenth century, a half-century after the Spanish discovered Indians using it in the Americas. In the twentieth century the British-American Tobacco Corporation enjoyed great success converting the Chinese into cigarette smokers.

55. Photographs of opium dens seemed as much in demand among Westerners as was a lurid popular literature describing them. The Chinaman's resort to opium became a standard feature in portrayals of an exotic East. Less was said in the West about the role of European and American merchants in promoting the sale of the drug to the Chinese.

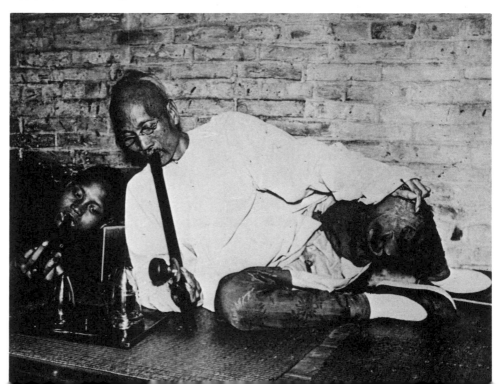

56. Men from Shanghai dressed for rain were the subject of this photograph of "Chinese types," which was made in a studio in the 1850s.

57, 58, 59. *Below and opposite.*
Very few could afford the great homes pictured on preceding pages. A farm family that was composed of two or three generations living together might hope to have a substantial dwelling like the one shown in the picture. Along the coast and on the larger rivers, thousands spent their entire lives on tiny boats such as those shown in the picture at top, opposite. In the bottom picture the houses of poor villagers can be glimpsed behind a ramshackle fence.

60. Marriage custom required that a bride dressed in her finery be transported from her own home to the groom's. The bride here is closed away from view in a red sedan chair that was rented for the occasion.

61. The finer details of weddings varied greatly from one region to another. Some of the men in this procession are wearing masks, whereas those in the preceding picture are not. Other contrasts are the open ricksha and the straw hats worn by the bridesmen.

62. Funerals, like weddings, varied according to region and family status. The heavy bier carried by a score of men, the lengthy procession of mourners, and the sedan chairs for the bereaved mark this as a ceremony for a person of importance. The ceremony, incidentally, is taking place in or near a foreign settlement. The sign on the left reads "Beware of Steam Roller."

63. White was the mourning color for the Chinese. These girls probably were not related to the deceased but were hired to make an impressive procession.

64, 65. The young son of the deceased walks in a procession (*right*) that is headed by priests (*below*).

66. *Opposite, top.* A funeral procession being formed outside the residence of a Westerner (note the teen-age girls in the background) will havé papier-mâché figures of servants, representing spirits to wait upon the deceased in the afterworld.

67. *Opposite, bottom.* Graves frequently were marked by simple tumuli and stones, as can be seen in the foreground in picture 113. In south China the more elaborate markers resembled stone armchairs of varying sizes. This is the grave of an unusually wealthy person.

68. Carpenters did all their work with a variety of small hand tools. This photograph shows two carpenters fashioning rough lumber, probably a beam for a house. Piles of roofing tile and bricks are in the background.

LIVELIHOODS

CHINESE society was overwhelmingly rural and poor. The ordinary farmhouse of central or northern China was a rude hovel of beaten earth thatched with straw. The living room doubled as granary, and furnishings were limited to a cheap table, two or three trestles for seats, a baby's cradle, and agricultural implements. In cotton-producing districts, there might also be a simple cotton gin, spinning wheel, or loom. Smaller livestock, such as pigs or chickens, were generally permitted to wander about the house, and larger animals often were tethered in an adjoining lean-to.

These were the results of an agricultural system that operated without the benefits of modern technology and science. Peasant farmers could till only a few acres, which they managed by marshaling every ounce of family energies. It was a system that required that about 80 percent of the people live close to the soil in rural villages. Annual yields were sufficiently large to support a population of more than 300 million, but there was little promise either of greater material abundance for the masses or of further economic development through industrialization.

One would scarcely guess the importance of China's peasant farmers from looking at old photographs. Photographers recorded people in other occupations—fishermen, petty merchants, and a variety of craftsmen—but they took few pictures of the people who composed the vast majority. Perhaps they were inhibited because, as outsiders, they did not enjoy easy access to China's rural society. More likely, as visitors from a West that was itself only recently industrialized, early photographers were not drawn to agricultural scenes.

69. Rice was the staple crop of south China. Seedlings were planted one at a time by hand after the paddy field had been carefully prepared. Terraced fields on hillsides might be irrigated by water flowing from above. On the flatlands, water was pumped into fields, sometimes by buffalo plodding in endless circles, but frequently by three or four persons turning a treadmill.

70. Ripe grain was cut with small sickles and carried to a hard floor of beaten earth for threshing. Here the grain was separated from the stalks with flails or a stone roller. Some peasants owned hand-powered fan mills for winnowing the grain; others tossed the grain and chaff into the wind. The pile of stalks to the left of the rice straw on this threshing floor indicates that these farmers produced more than a single crop. In the background is a bamboo grove that would yield edible shoots and wood that could be used in an infinite number of ways.

71. Annual yields north of the Yangtze were slimmer than those in the south. The climate permitted the planting of only a single crop each year, instead of two or three. Wheat and millet, not rice, were the staples, and they were raised without irrigation. The simple plow used by this northern farmer was not markedly different from the one used in the south. Here donkeys furnished the power; in the south, buffalo were the draft animals.

72. Newly transplanted tea bushes dot this Fukien hillside, overlooking fields of rice. Like other farm crops, tea was raised on small farms and tended with family labor. It, too, was a labor-intensive crop. Tea leaves were plucked carefully from the plant three to five times each year and transported by the farmer to market. Hand labor was employed again in the final processing.

73. Most ducks that reached Chinese tables came from farms. However, these young hunters made their living by shooting the wild birds with muzzle-loading guns.

74. *Opposite*. Large dip nets, which were secured by pulleys to bamboo frames and operated by winches, were lowered repeatedly into shallow waters and then raised quickly to capture any fish that had ventured over the netting. The boatman's job was to take the fish out of the net. To attract fish to the area, the fishermen sometimes baited the cords of the net by rubbing them with egg-whites.

75. *Below*. These fishermen work their dredgelike nets through the mud to catch marine life in the bottom waters. The regularly spaced mounds in the background contain dirt that could be spread to raise the levee.

76, 77. Commercial fishing on a somewhat larger scale was common along China's coast. Small boats, usually operating in pairs, ventured out short distances beyond the shore to drag nets. The catch was then dried and salted before marketing.

78. The Shanghai women who have been grouped for this picture are embroidering cloth held in wooden frames. They were employed by one of the many small firms scattered through China that specialized in native products —jades, brasswork, lacquerware, cloisonné, or silks. Local specialties were likely to have been determined by the resources of the area. Fine porcelains could be made from the clay of Kiangsi Province, whereas Peking's famous rugs resulted partly from that city's easy access to the wool of China's borderlands.

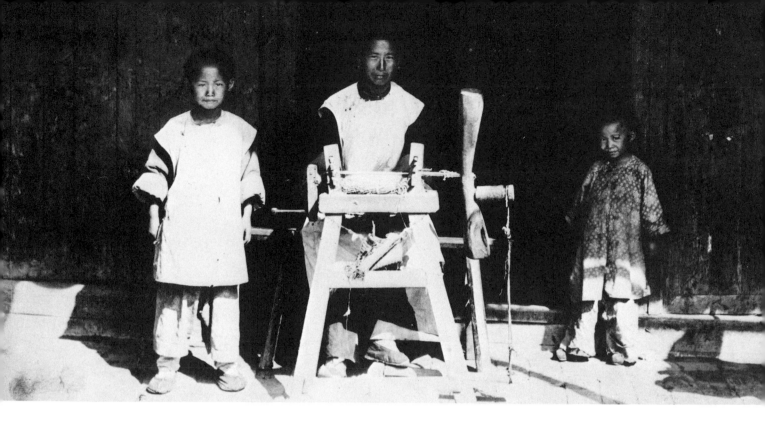

79, 80. The production of cotton textiles was an important cottage industry in regions where cotton was grown. Above, a woman is operating a foot-powered cotton gin; below, another is spinning. When modern textile machinery was introduced into China, peasants who specialized in ginning and spinning were the first to suffer a loss of income. Hand looms, which produced a fabric that was peculiarly suited to popular needs, were not immediately supplanted by modern machines.

81. Home delivery of water was available to those who could afford the service. Custom held that water should be drunk hot after it was boiled. This was a practice followed even by the poor, who could not afford to add tea leaves to the hot water. This picture, showing how water was obtained, amply illustrates the wisdom behind the custom.

82. Vendors selling food and drink were a common sight on city streets. This woman may have been selling some kind of herbal beverage. She does not seem to have had a little charcoal stove, an essential part of a tea seller's equipment.

83, 84. Craftsmen, such as the mender of porcelains (*above*) and the cobbler (*below*) made regular rounds in cities. All that they needed in their work was contained in boxes suspended at the ends of a carrying pole. Unless they were expected, they did not stop at each place along the way but rather announced their arrival with distinctive cries or by beating a special noisemaker.

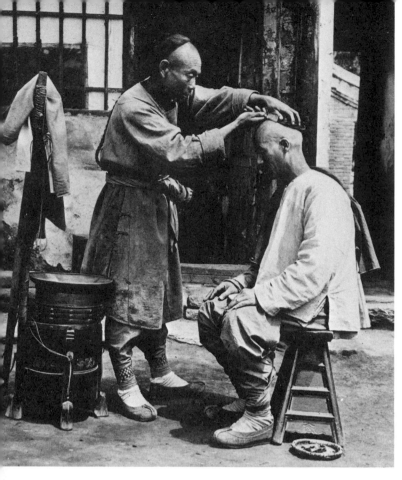

85. The peripatetic barber disappeared after the Manchu Dynasty was overthrown in 1911 and Chinese were no longer required to wear the queue as a sign of submission. Since the style required that every part of the head except the crown be shaved, frequent barbering was necessary. Even on the street, a customer could get the full treatment. The stool on which this man sits has drawers for the barber's tools, and the water in the basin on the left is heated with a few lumps of charcoal. If a man were growing bald, the barber could furnish false hair to fill out a wispy queue.

86. This studio pose, showing a physiognomist at work, has the look of a caricature. The art of divining one's fortunes from a study of facial characteristics was no joke to the Chinese mind, however. A physiognomist who had established a reputation for accuracy could expect brisk patronage.

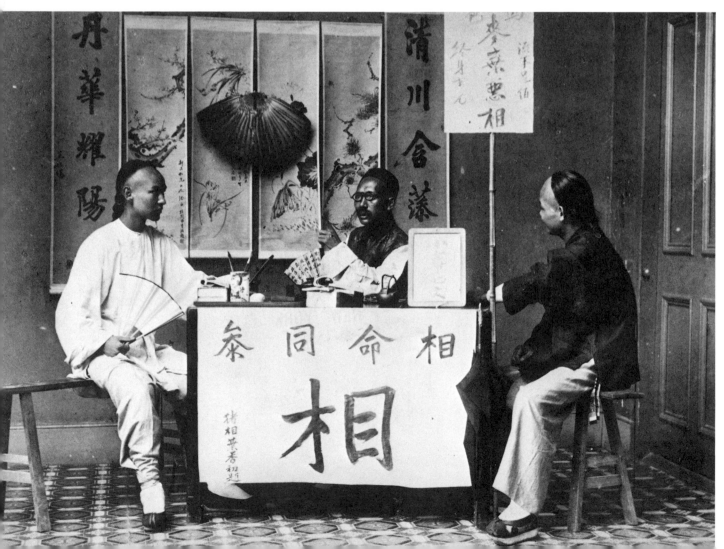

87. Floriculture was an amazingly well-developed industry. Florists not only produced plants for sale but also vied with one another in breeding new specimens. The care lavished on plants was based on a long tradition of serious botanical studies. Although the Chinese esteemed plants for their beauty, they also had long known their value as medicines. Much of China's early science focused on assessing the properties of various species.

88. *Overleaf.* The fire-fighting company organized by Shanghai's silk guild for the protection of its members' property was considerably better equipped than most volunteer groups. Moreover, a Western advisor, dressed in Chinese garb, perhaps employed to instruct the company in the use of the imported fire wagon, stands in the background.

89. This lifeboat was the property of a rescue squad in a coastal town. The government collected taxes from businesses but otherwise kept its distance. Officials neither subscribed to doctrines of economic development nor believed that anything was owed to the farmer or merchant other than the maintenance of order. This laissez-faire philosophy meant that Chinese had to organize as volunteers to provide themselves with vital services.

COMMUNICATION

THE geographic horizons of the common people were limited. It was not uncommon for a person to live an entire lifetime without venturing more than a few miles beyond his native village. Moreover, little influence from the outside world was likely to have filtered into rural villages, except those near foreign settlements on the east coast, before the end of the nineteenth century. It was this parochialism that encouraged the regional variations in clothing, diet, customs, and architectural design that have been so apparent in these photographs. Even the Chinese language reflected the immobility of the populace. Although the written word was standardized and the Peking dialect was known to all educated Chinese, there was in fact no commonly understood popular language. Local dialects varied so greatly that people living only a few miles apart often could not communicate.

From this it should not be inferred that old China lacked transportation. On the contrary, her waterways and roads were equal to the best of those in other preindustrial societies. The eastern and most densely populated area was served by canals that connected numerous rivers and lakes. Navigable waters reached deep into the interior, and where there was no water, roads had been constructed. The system enabled the imperial government to move its officials about and to stay in touch with a vast domain. It also permitted a rather substantial internal trade. Travel was slow and uncomfortable, however, and a practice large numbers of people avoided.

90. Wheelbarrows constructed along these lines were superbly designed for the narrow paths that served as roads for local traffic. Some barrows had handles in front as well as in back, permitting a second man to help with the load, but a vehicle such as this could transport upward of five hundred pounds.

91. The ricksha—or, more properly, *jinrikisha* (human-powered cart)—was a Japanese invention of the 1860s that combined Western-style wheels with Asian muscle power. Since it proved extremely useful under nineteenth-century conditions, its use spread to China and other Asian countries. Years later the ricksha was modified with the addition of half of a chain-driven bicycle to the front. The result was the pedicab. Old-style rickshas survive today only as tourist attractions in Hong Kong.

92. Some of the paths in the western mountains were so primitive that no vehicular traffic was possible. Human cargo carriers surmounted these conditions, shouldering all manner of freight—including an occasional human passenger. The steep terrain must have made the work harrowing, and the heavy loads soon destroyed the health of the carrier.

93. Sedan chairs, as shown on page 76, were carried on poles by either two or four men and served as transportation for Chinese of rank and for foreigners. Here the sedan chair has been enlarged to accommodate more than one person and adapted so that it can be carried by animals in terrain too rough for wheels.

94. The reinforced axles and spokeless wheels of Chinese wagons were designed to withstand the strains and upsets that were common on bad roads. Since there were no springs, passengers took such comfort as they could from cotton-filled pads laid on the floor of the cart.

95. Like the ricksha, this freight wagon used Western wheels. As long as the roads were in reasonably good repair, the lighter weight of such wagons recommended them over those of native design.

96. Carts for freight that was to be transported over some distance were drawn by three or four horses or donkeys, usually driven in tandem with one remaining within the wagon's shafts, as can be seen here. Animals, like their masters, suffered from disease and the scarcity of food.

97. These bales of tea bricks were bulky but apparently not too heavy for single draft animals. Note the woman and children peeking from the doorway.

98. On the plains of Manchuria, the wind could assist with the transportation of heavy loads of munitions. This picture is undated but apparently was made around 1900, at a time when both Manchuria and Korea were the prizes in great international rivalries.

99. The northern terminus of the Grand Canal was a channel that passed alongside Peking's great city wall. The tower of the eastern gate may be seen in the distant background. Here camel trains from China's northern borderlands met to exchange goods with canal boats bringing freight from the south.

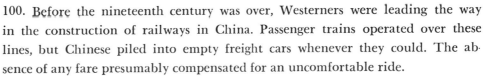

100. Before the nineteenth century was over, Westerners were leading the way in the construction of railways in China. Passenger trains operated over these lines, but Chinese piled into empty freight cars whenever they could. The absence of any fare presumably compensated for an uncomfortable ride.

101. *Overleaf.* The heavy logs and building stone seen piled here emphasize the importance of canals in China's transportation system. The boat dwellings on the canal and the family wash visible hanging outside the buildings behind the piled lumber are still another illustration of the integration of family and commercial life.

102. The northern portion of the Grand Canal, which reached from Peking to the Huai River, was built by the Yuan Dynasty in the thirteenth century. It connected with a network of older canals, thereby linking the capital with Canton. Early in the nineteenth century it was capable of carrying more than six thousand grain barges, each of which was about eighty feet long and transported forty-five tons. By the second half of the century, it had deteriorated badly, and only short links such as this one were open to traffic.

103. *Below.* Canal boats were not of uniform design. However, virtually all of them served not just as commercial vessels but as homes. The bargelike design of these boats enabled them to carry either freight or passengers. The awning protected the cargo and served as the family's rooftop.

104. *Opposite.* The striped sail identifies this vessel as a government craft. Such vessels were used by the revenue bureau for the collection of taxes. Larger vessels were operated by the imperial government for the transportation of salt, the sale of which was an official monopoly, and for the apprehension of smugglers. China had virtually no seagoing navy of the type that was common in the West.

105. By the 1860s steamboats had been introduced in China's coastal and river shipping. An American firm, Russell and Company, pioneered in this enterprise. Competition soon came from British and Chinese firms. This steamer plied the Yangtze River carrying passengers and freight.

Honam — Canton

106. Before the first treaties were signed, Westerners were confined to fifteen acres on the outskirts of Canton. The treaties permitted foreigners to venture into the city itself and to enjoy the relatively spacious regions behind these buildings on Honam Island. Here Western residents could escape the Chinese and the business of their riverfront offices by strolling in the fields.

TREATY PORTS

THE Westerners who took these early photographs were themselves a conspicuous part of the Chinese scene. Along the China coast during the second half of the nineteenth century, Europeans and Americans built communities that resembled those they had left behind. In his book *Illustrations of China and Its People*, published in 1873, John Thomson, the noted British photographer, recalled the contrasts between them and the surrounding Chinese cities:

> Shanghai . . . [is] the greatest of the treaty ports of China, where, within a few years, a foreign settlement has sprung up on the banks of Woosong of such vast proportions as to lead a visitor to fancy that he has been suddenly transported to one of our great English ports; the crowd of shipping, the wharves, warehouses, and landing-stages, the stone embankment, the elegance and costliness of the buildings, the noise of constant traffic in the streets, the busy roads smooth as a billiard-table, and the well-kept garden that skirts the river affording evidence of foreign taste and refinement, all tending to aid the illusion. One only, however, has to drive beyond the foreign settlement to dispel the dream, and to find the native dwellings huddled together, as if pressed back to make way for a higher civilization that has planted a city in their midst.

Thomson might have added that the differences reached beyond appearances. Within the confines of their tight little communities, Westerners lived almost untouched by the influences of Chinese traditions.

The presence of these Western communities on Chinese soil was a product of Peking's capitulation to mounting Western pressures. As late as 1839, China could require Americans and Western

Europeans (Russians were under separate control) to trade only at Canton and to conduct themselves as Chinese authorities might prescribe. Then China reeled under the dual impact of internal upheaval and defeat in wars with the West. In treaties phrased so that foreigners shared the spoils, China made important concessions: an ever-increasing number of cities were to be opened to foreign trade and residence (hence the name *treaty ports*); foreign citizens were to be exempt from Chinese law under a system known as extraterritoriality; and foreign governments were to be permitted to regulate China's tariff. It was a system that allowed foreign governments to dominate the Western enclaves while the Chinese monarchy continued to rule the broad interior of the empire as a whole. As an expedient that satisfied immediate foreign demands and thereby relieved pressures on the dynasty, the treaty ports were acceptable to China's imperial government. China's modern patriots, however, were enraged by the foreign privileges represented by the treaty ports. As China's revolution gained momentum in this century, the treaty ports and the life-styles that had been fashioned within them were to be swept away.

107. *Opposite*. Canton had been the center of China's trade with the West for a century before the signature in 1842–44 of treaties formalizing relations with Europe and America. A dozen Cantonese firms formed a guild known as the Co-hong, which funneled merchandise collected in south and central China to Westerners who were permitted to erect "factories" (really offices and warehouses) in the Shameen region of the riverfront shown in this picture.

108. *Below*. The ruins of these great warehouses for shipping tea testify both to the importance of that product in China's foreign trade and to the constant danger of fire in Canton's congested buildings. Foreign merchants suffered from destructive fires in 1822, 1842, and 1843; all of their buildings were burned in 1856, but trade was so lucrative that everything was quickly rebuilt. As early as 1800, 20 million pounds of tea, which had eclipsed exports of silk and porcelains, were passing through Canton annually.

109. *Overleaf*. Foochow was a picturesque city of considerable size and consequence before its designation in 1842 as one of the five original treaty ports. It was the headquarters of Manchu civil and military officialdom in Fukien Province. Its location on the Min River, which flowed through a major tea-producing district, and its excellent harbor gave the city additional importance as a port. This panorama of the city faces Temple Hill, a noted landmark.

110. *Opposite.* By 1880, Hong Kong boasted a population of 130,000—mostly Chinese—and many elegant new buildings on Victoria Peak, which rose more than eighteen hundred feet above one of the world's most beautiful harbors. The island itself was barren and unpromising when it was ceded to the British in 1842. Great Britain set to work immediately to make the rock an indispensable base for its China trade.

111. Pagoda Anchorage, a spacious area in the Min River pictured here at low tide, served as Foochow's port. It was thirty miles from the ocean and about seven miles downriver from the city. Along the banks of the anchorage, the Chinese built an arsenal for manufacturing modern gunboats, and Western merchants located a small residential district for themselves.

112. *Opposite, top.* The main foreign settlement at Foochow was situated on an island in the Min River. In the foreground is the Foochow city wall, and beyond it are large foreign residences and an Anglican church.

113. *Opposite, bottom.* A closer view of the foreign residences at Foochow reveals that they had been built in the midst of an old Chinese burial ground. The imposing house on the left with a gazebo behind it housed the representative of the Anglican church, which also was situated in the burial ground. Rather substantial payments reportedly were made to the Chinese to quiet outcries against the foreigners' desecration of the graves.

114. The Western settlement at Foochow had no racecourse, but it did have bowling alleys and these "fives" courts ("fives" was a game similar to handball).

115. Shanghai's location on the Wusung River and its ready access to the Yangtze, which ran deep into the interior, and to the Grand Canal, which stretched north and south, had made it an important center of domestic trade. When the city was opened to foreign commerce in 1843, Chinese and foreign capital flowed into the area, touching off a building boom that soon made Shanghai the largest and most important of the treaty ports. The foreign settlement was built in what had been a swamp dotted with a few fishermen's huts. This photograph was made in 1870.

116. This view of the Shanghai settlement in 1900 illustrates how dramatically the foreign community had grown in less than sixty years. Although a great many Chinese lived and worked in this area, they were beyond the jurisdiction of their native government. After 1854 the Shanghai settlement was governed by an exclusively foreign municipal council.

117. *Opposite*. The flag marks the American consulate in Shanghai. Only the rickshas identify this street as being in China.

118. The headquarters of the Chinese Maritime Customs Administration was located in Shanghai and housed in this Western-style building, which symbolized China's decline into semicolonial status. Under the treaties of 1842–44, China had ceded to foreign powers the right to regulate its customs rates, and during the breakdown in governmental activity that was precipitated by the T'ai-p'ing Rebellion in the 1850s, Peking agreed to the establishment of the Maritime Customs Administration, an agency nominally Chinese but actually run by foreigners.

119. The mixture of foreigners and Chinese in the enterprise of the Shanghai settlement was to be seen everywhere. These Chinese laborers were photographed tamping the earth for the foundations of a building on the famous waterfront bund.

120, 121. *Opposite*. These Chinese catered to foreign customers. The earthen jars were commonly used utility vessels, but the coal-fired space heaters and the tin bathtub, seen hanging on the wall at the left (*top*), were certainly produced for Westerners. The open stalls of the Hongkew market (*bottom*) offered vegetables for Western tables.

122. Chinese worked under a foreigner's supervision in the tea-tasting room of George H. Macy and Company. The drape overhead was rigged to fan the air on hot summer days.

123. This tea-processing firm was identified with a Chinese name but was located in the foreign settlement. Here tea was pressed into bricks, probably for the Russian market.

124. The wheelbarrows so common in central China were used to transport imported kerosene at this unidentified Shanghai factory.

125. Business enterprise was not the only undertaking in which Westerners and Chinese mixed. Here two foreign professors, who were probably on the faculty of a Christian missionary college, pose with a Chinese colleague and their students.

126. *Opposite, top*. Traffic on the Shanghai bund revealed not only the bustling activity of the foreign settlement but also its cosmopolitan character. The wide, paved, tree-lined street was fronted by buildings that might have been lifted out of any number of Western cities. A turbaned Indian directs traffic while Chinese go about their business.

127. *Opposite, bottom*. Elsewhere in the foreign settlement a policeman is dressed in a Western uniform, and a telephone line is strung on poles at the left. Most of the people on the street appear to be Chinese. The vehicle on the right appears to be an updated model of a night-soil collector's wagon.

128. These Chinese chained together and guarded by police under the supervision of a white-garbed Westerner on the left indicate foreign authority in the Shanghai settlement. The prisoners have been brought out to repair the streets.

129. In this portrait made on the veranda of Russell and Company's offices, Frank Blackwell Forbes (1839–1908) stands on the right. Although Forbes's steamship enterprise eventually could not withstand the competition mounted by heavily capitalized Chinese, he and his associates displayed unusual imagination and managerial skill in building East Asia's first large, modern, merchant fleet.

130. Russell and Company, an American firm whose offices are shown here, had pioneered in the American tea trade at Canton and managed a steamship line that dominated traffic on the Yangtze River during the 1860s. The capital to organize the steamship line was drawn in roughly equal portions from Russell and Company partners in the United States, foreign merchants in China, and Chinese investors.

131, 132. The possibilities for adapting an elegant Western life-style to China are dramatized in these views of the house and lawn belonging to Frank Blackwell Forbes, a partner in Russell and Company who was responsible for managing the firm's steamship line. Note the household servants and Chinese nurse who are portrayed along with the family.

133. This Shanghai country club was out of bounds for Chinese, who were only allowed to enter such places as servants.

134. *Overleaf*. Inside the great Western-style houses one was likely to discover a blend of Victorian and Chinese decor. The tables in the foreground were probably constructed to special order by Chinese craftsmen. They were elaborately ornamented in Chinese fashion, but their style recalled Western pieces that were common in the era.

135, 136. *Above, opposite.* The horses and riders speeding around a beautifully manicured race track and the top-hatted gentlemen and fashionably dressed ladies packing the stands were photographed in Shanghai.

137. By the end of the nineteenth century, Christian missionaries were building churches to attract Chinese converts, but this large church in Shanghai was only for Westerners.

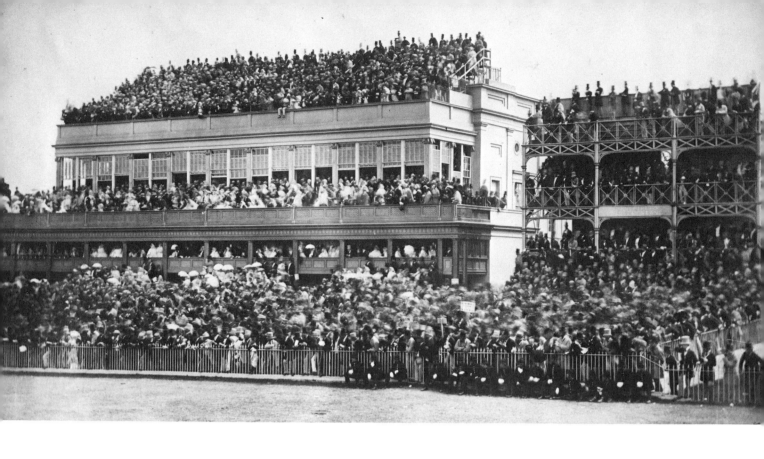

138, 139. *Overleaf.* The Shanghai Settlement's park, with its bandstand, greenhouse to display exotic plants, and pleasant walkways, was still another place from which Chinese were excluded. In later years, Chinese nationalists were to employ in their antiforeign campaigns the sign on the park entrances that read "No dogs or Chinese allowed."

140. Railways were slow to develop because they invaded everyday Chinese life by crossing canals and rice fields, disturbing grave mounds, and adversely affecting the spirits of the wind and water, in which there was great popular faith. A small, unauthorized Shanghai–Wusung line was built by foreigners in 1876, only to be purchased and destroyed by Chinese the following year. Several years later this line connecting Shanghai with Wusung and other points was built.

141. The sportily attired ladies on a summer outing to visit the eastern terminus of the Great Wall have probably traveled from Peking.

142. Foreign travelers occasionally could find a Western hotel that relieved them of the hazards of a Chinese inn. This hotel in Peking was run by a French national. It was to be destroyed in the Boxer Rebellion, 1900.

143. China was hardly equipped to serve Western tourists. Even so, some sightseeing could be done in style. The two well-dressed gentlemen and their Chinese guide are shown leaving a watchtower on Canton's city wall known as the Five-Storied Pagoda. The building was undistinguished and was not even a real pagoda, but tourists inevitably went there by sedan chairs because it was the best spot for viewing the city.

144. Manchu "banner men," such as the one pictured here, were considered the Ch'ing Dynasty's first line of defense. After China's defeat in the Arrow War, a few thousand of these troops were given modern arms and training. In general, however, officers were still chosen by an examination that tested their skills in mounted and dismounted archery, sword brandishing, pulling a powerful bow, and lifting a heavy stone.

CHINA'S RESPONSES

THE Ch'ing Dynasty proved incapable of formulating a consistent policy for dealing with foreign penetration. Peking initially was not much concerned by the approach of the West. The Western merchants who led the way to China offered trade that was profitable to the Chinese, and China's power was such that the foreign merchants could easily be controlled at Canton. It was only when Westerners insisted on extending their activities beyond Canton and applying their own rules that the Chinese became alarmed. They believed at first that they could solve the problem either by punishing the foreign barbarians or by conciliating them. Neither approach worked. The attempted punishments resulted in defeats in two wars, the so-called Opium War (1839–41) and the Arrow War (1858–60), and the gentler pressures of conciliation failed utterly to persuade foreigners to abandon their expansionist aims. Thereafter, Peking resorted to a double-edged policy. It accepted the treaties giving foreigners special privileges because they relieved immediate foreign pressures. At the same time it adopted a policy of "self-strengthening" that aimed at the eventual development of resources for conquering the foreign menace.

Meanwhile, popular feelings ran to opposite extremes. In every treaty port or wherever missionaries worked, there were Chinese who formed cordial relationships with the outsiders. Among such Chinese, foreigners were perceived as the source of profits or as a people proclaiming a better way of life. Yet an increasingly vehement antiforeign sentiment also arose and took the form of rioting against missionaries. In 1900 northern China was rocked by a violent outburst known as the Boxer Rebellion. This movement, like the antimissionary riots, was aimed at driving foreigners from China, but neither had any chance of success. Indeed, their immediate result was to give the powers opportunities to make new demands on China. Another half century was to elapse before China could shake free of her semicolonial status.

145. This marble picnic pavilion, which was built by the Ch'ing court with funds that originally had been allocated for the construction of modern naval vessels, symbolized the troubles that soon overtook "self-strengthening." China, it seemed, would not be saved with reforms that failed to effect fundamental transformations in the whole society.

146. By the second half of the nineteenth century, there was no unified command of Chinese troops, and the troops themselves presented no uniformity in training or equipment. This straggling line of uniformed men was identified only as imperial forces. They appear to be armed solely with antiquated rifles.

147. "Self-strengthening" was based on the theory that China could equip herself with modern arms without undergoing any fundamental reforms. This arsenal at Tientsin manufactured gunpowder and built modern gunboats. It was one of several constructed along the China coast.

148. European or American instructors were hired by China's "self-strengtheners" to teach the Chinese how to build and use arms. This gun crew at the Shanghai arsenal was commanded by a Westerner, who stands in the right background.

149. The Chinese dead and the destroyed fortifications at the Taku forts guarding the approaches to Peking indicated what was in store for China. This destruction was at the hands of British and French forces invading China during the Arrow War.

150, 151. *Overleaf.* Germany capitalized on China's weakness by concluding in 1898 an agreement that provided for the establishment of a base for German armed forces at Kiaochow Bay and for special privileges in a German sphere of influence in Shantung. The buildings within the compound wall are German barracks at the edge of Kiaochow Bay (*below*). Nearby, German troops parade on Chinese soil (*overleaf*).

152. *Opposite*. The outbreak of the Boxer Rebellion in 1900 precipitated mobilization of all available foreign manpower in China. In Shanghai five thousand volunteers lined up for a review on the racetrack. Note in the foreground the uniformed Chinese who have come to watch the show.

153. *Right*. Foreign powers reacted to the Boxer Rebellion by sending troops to China to protect the lives and property of their nationals. Black cavalrymen from the United States are seen riding down a street in Tientsin.

154. *Below*. Somewhere in north China, Russian troops march off a ship.

155, 156. In Shanghai, Indian Sikhs under British command prepare "tiffin," or lunch (*above*), and a British official confers with a native officer of the second Rajputs (*left*).

157. German general Count Alfred von Waldersee was given command of an international force organized to march to the rescue of foreigners under siege in the legation quarter of Peking. He is shown being welcomed here when he arrived in northern China, but by the time he arrived, the forces had already accomplished their rescue mission.

158. In Peking, near the walls of the Imperial City, the Boxers besieged the foreign legation quarter, where 475 foreign civilians, 450 guards from eight nations, and perhaps 3,000 Chinese Christians were wedged into an area about three-quarters of a mile square. Sometimes Chinese laborers were allowed to bring food through the lines to those under siege.

159. Indian troops, who were the first to break through Boxer lines, were photographed carrying a wounded comrade in a covered litter.

160, 161. These two photographs portray the physical damage caused by the fighting and looting that followed the evacuation of the legation quarter.

162. The Boxers took several hundred foreign lives. In Wei-hai-wei, wounded British sailors pose on hospital steps.

163. Other photographs, though, leave little doubt that the Boxer Rebellion resulted in tragedy for China. Western troops marched off with captured Chinese battle flags.

164. Victorious, a mounted Western sailor rides serenely down a street in Tientsin.

165. Along the Tientsin bund the British gunboat H.M.S. *Firebrand* remained anchored throughout the winter of 1900–1901 for the protection of foreign residents.